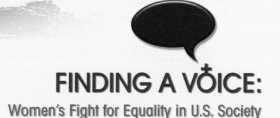

FINDING A VOICE:
Women's Fight for Equality in U.S. Society

WOMEN GO TO WORK: 1941–1945

DONNA ROPPELT

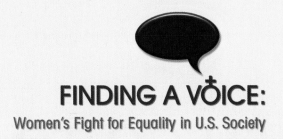

FINDING A VOICE:

Women's Fight for Equality in U.S. Society

TITLES IN THIS SERIES

A WOMAN'S PLACE IN EARLY AMERICA

ORIGINS OF THE WOMEN'S RIGHTS MOVEMENT

SEEKING THE RIGHT TO VOTE

WOMEN'S RIGHTS ON THE FRONTIER

THE EQUAL RIGHTS AMENDMENT

WOMEN GO TO WORK, 1941–45

WOMEN IN THE CIVIL RIGHTS MOVEMENT

THE WOMEN'S LIBERATION MOVEMENT, 1960–1990

THE FEMINIST MOVEMENT TODAY

FINDING A VOICE:
Women's Fight for Equality in U.S. Society

WOMEN GO TO WORK: 1941–1945

DONNA ROPPELT

MASON CREST
PHILADELPHIA

Mason Crest
370 Reed Road, Suite 302
Broomall, PA 19008
www.MasonCrest.com

Printed and bound in the United States of America.

CPSIA Compliance Information: Batch #FF2012-6. For further information, contact Mason Crest at 1-866-MCP-Book.

First printing
1 3 5 7 9 8 6 4 2

Library of Congress Cataloging-in-Publication Data

Roppelt, Donna.
  Women go to work, 1941-1945 / Donna Roppelt.
    p. cm. — (Finding a voice : women's fight for equality in U.S. society)
  Includes bibliographical references and index.
  ISBN 978-1-4222-2357-4 (hc)
  ISBN 978-1-4222-2367-3 (pb)
  1. Women—Employment—United States—History—20th century—Juvenile
literature. 2. Women—United States—Economic conditions—20th century—
Juvenile literature. 3. World War, 1939-1945—Women—United States—Juvenile
literature. I. Title.
  HD6095.R72 2012
  331.40973'09044—dc23
                                    2011043483

Publisher's note: All quotations in this book are taken from original sources, and contain the spelling and grammatical inconsistencies of the original texts.

Picture credits: Library of Congress: 11, 20, 23, 28, 29, 30, 32, 36 (top, bottom right), 38, 39, 44; National Archives and Records Administration: 3, 8, 12, 18, 21, 26, 34, 36 (bottom left), 40, 47; Mort Kunstler/National Guard Heritage Series: 16; NY Daily News via Getty Images: 15; © 2011 Photos.com, a division of Getty Images: 54; U.S. Air Force photo: 45, 46; U.S. Army photo: 42, 49; U.S. Navy photo: 43, 53.

TABLE OF CONTENTS

Introduction   6

1   We Can Do It!   9

2   The Women at Home   17

3   Women Volunteer   25

4   Rosie the Riveter, Wanda the Welder, and More   31

5   Women in the Services   41

6   After the War   50

    Chapter Notes   56
    Chronology   58
    Further Reading   59
    Internet Resources   60
    Glossary   61
    Index   62
    Contributors   64

INTRODUCTION

As the Executive Director of the Sewall-Belmont House & Museum, which is the fifth and final headquarters of the historic National Woman's Party (NWP), I am surrounded each day by artifacts that give voice to the stories of Alice Paul, Lucy Burns, Doris Stevens, Alva Belmont, and the whole community of women who waged an intense campaign for the right to vote during the second decade of the 20th century. The original photographs, documents, protest banners, and magnificent floor-length capes worn by these courageous activists during marches and demonstrations help us bring their work to life for the many groups who tour the museum each week.

A. Page Harrington, director, Sewall-Belmont House & Museum

The perseverance of the suffragists bore fruit in 1920, with the ratification of the 19th Amendment. It was a huge milestone, though certainly not the end of the journey toward full equality for American women.

Throughout much (if not most) of American history, social conventions and the law constrained female participation in the political, economic, and intellectual life of the nation. Women's voices were routinely stifled, their contributions downplayed or dismissed, their potential ignored. Underpinning this state of affairs was a widely held assumption of male superiority in most spheres of human endeavor.

Always, however, there were women who gave the lie to gender-based stereotypes. Some helped set the national agenda. For example, in the years preceding the Revolutionary War, Mercy Otis Warren made a compelling case for American independence through her writings. Abigail Adams, every bit the intellectual equal of her husband, counseled John Adams to "remember the ladies and be more generous and favorable to them than your ancestors" when creating laws for the new country. Sojourner Truth helped lead the movement to abolish slavery in the 19th century. A hundred years later, Rosa Parks galvanized the civil rights movement, which finally secured for African Americans the promise of equality under the law.

The lives of these women are familiar today. So, too, are the stories of groundbreakers such as astronaut Sally Ride; Supreme Court justice Sandra Day O'Connor; and Nancy Pelosi, Speaker of the House of Representatives.

But famous figures are only part of the story. The path toward gender equality was also paved—and American society shaped—by countless women whose individual lives and deeds have never been chronicled in depth. These include the women who toiled alongside their fathers and brothers and husbands on the western frontier; the women who kept U.S. factories running during World War II; and the women who worked tirelessly to promote the goals of the modern feminist movement.

The FINDING A VOICE series tells the stories of famous and anonymous women alike. Together these volumes provide a wide-ranging overview of American women's long quest to achieve full equality with men—a quest that continues today.

The Sewall-Belmont House & Museum is located at 144 Constitution Avenue in Washington, D.C. You can find out more on the Web at www.sewallbelmont.org

1

WE CAN DO IT!

You've seen the picture. On a bright yellow background, a young woman is rolling up the sleeve of her blue shirt to show her arm muscle. She is wearing makeup, and her eyebrows are neatly plucked. But her gaze is direct and resolute. She exudes determination. That sense is reinforced by the words floating over the red polka-dot scarf that covers the woman's hair: "We Can Do It!"

Just what is this woman so determined to do? The short answer is factory work. But her ultimate aim is much, much bigger than simply holding down a job on an assembly line. She means to help her country in a time of desperate need.

The image of the blue-shirted, biceps-baring woman became an important symbol. It represented the strength and can-do spirit of the millions of American women who went to work in American factories between 1941 and 1945.

WOMEN IN THE WORKPLACE

At the start of the 20th century, one in five Americans employed outside the home was female. By the 1920s, the number had risen to one in four.

But women were limited to certain kinds of jobs considered appropriate for their gender. They were teachers, nurses, and social workers. They worked in offices as secretaries and clerks. They worked in retail stores as sales-people. They were domestics, cooking and cleaning in other people's homes. Women did work in factories, just not in heavy industries such as automobile manufacturing. Rather, they sewed clothing, assembled shoes, canned food, and held other domestic jobs.

The 1930s were very difficult for workers, male and female alike. This was a period known as the Great Depression. The world economy had col-lapsed. Thousands of American banks failed. Tens of thousands of factories and businesses closed. Millions of Americans lost their jobs. In 1932 and 1933, the worst years of the Depression, nearly one in every four American workers was unemployed.

THE SHADOW OF WAR

By 1940–41, the U.S. economy was coming out of the Depression. There were several reasons for this. One of them was World War II.

The war started in September 1939. On the first of that month, Nazi Germany invaded Poland. Two days later, Great Britain and France declared war on Germany. Great Britain, France, and other countries that fought on their side were known as the Allies.

FAST FACT

During the Depression, married women who worked were often criticized for being selfish. Many people said that men should get any available jobs because they were the breadwinners for families. This idea was misguided. Many mar-ried women had to support their families after their husbands were laid off. Plus, many of the jobs they found were in traditionally female fields. Men weren't prepared to take these jobs.

Scenes of the Great Depression, a period of economic hard times that lasted from 1929 until the early 1940s. (Top) Unemployed men and women line up for government relief supplies in Arizona. (Right) This iconic 1936 photo of a destitute woman with seven children in a camp for migrant workers in Nipomo, California, reflects the despair many Americans felt during the Great Depression.

The United States was officially neutral. That means it didn't take sides in the war. But President Franklin D. Roosevelt believed that Germany had to be stopped. He also thought that the United States might one day be pulled into the war. Roosevelt convinced the U.S. Congress to pass a bill that would allow the Allies to buy American-made weapons.

In early 1940, German forces took Belgium, the Netherlands, Luxembourg, and Denmark. France surrendered in June. But Great Britain held out.

The rise of aggressive dictators like Adolf Hitler in Germany during the 1930s led to the outbreak of the Second World War.

Meanwhile, Italy had joined the war on Germany's side. And in September 1940, Japan—which had invaded China—became an ally of Germany and Italy. Together, the three countries were called the Axis powers.

On December 29, 1940, President Roosevelt spoke to the nation over the radio. Some Americans, he pointed out, thought the Axis powers would never want to attack the United States. The president said this was a foolish notion. He said the Axis dictatorships wanted to "dominate and enslave the human race." If they could, they would eventually strike the United States, Roosevelt said. The president claimed that the best way to prevent this was to make the country a "great arsenal of democracy." Vast quantities of military equipment needed to be manufactured. And this needed to be done quickly, Roosevelt said.

The military buildup would make the United States stronger. The country would be better able to defend itself.

But much of the military equipment made in the United States would be sent to Great Britain. Roosevelt said that the British and other free peoples fighting the Axis were also helping to protect America's security.

There was one problem, though. Britain no longer had enough money to pay for supplies. So, in March 1941, Roosevelt signed into law the Lend-

Lease Act. It allowed military equipment, food, and other supplies to be sent to any nation fighting on the side of the Allies. No immediate payment would be required.

BOOM TIME

The American economy had already begun to recover from the Depression. But Lend-Lease led to a boom. Businesses expanded. Assembly lines buzzed with activity. Shipyards raced to fill orders for new vessels. And millions of Americans who couldn't find work during the Depression now had well-paying jobs.

Industrial production was geared toward war. That meant factories across the country had to retool. Factories that had made goods such as cars, refrigerators, or sewing machines were set up to produce airplanes, tanks, and guns. The work was physically demanding and often dangerous. And it was done by men.

The fighting in World War II expanded in 1941. British and German forces battled in North Africa and the Middle East. Germany invaded Yugoslavia and Greece. Its forces pushed into the Baltic Sea region. And, in June, Germany launched a massive invasion of the Soviet Union.

Many Americans still hoped that the United States wouldn't become involved in the fighting. But that hope was shattered one Sunday in December.

NEEDED: AMERICAN WOMEN

On the morning of December 7, 1941, hundreds of Japanese warplanes took off from aircraft carriers in the waters north of Hawaii. They pounded the American naval base at Pearl Harbor. The surprise attack sank or damaged 18 U.S. ships. It also killed more than 2,400 people.

The next day, Congress approved a declaration of war on Japan. On December 11, Germany and Italy, Japan's Axis partners, declared war on the United States.

Millions of American men would be needed to fight in the war. A great many of them would be leaving civilian jobs. The question was, who would do these jobs when the men entered the armed services? Clearly, American women would have to take on a larger role in the workforce.

They would also have to take on a different role. They would have to do jobs that had always been considered "men's work." The country couldn't

THE ORIGINAL ROSIE

Many people associate Rosie the Riveter with the young woman in the popular "We Can Do It!" poster (pictured on page 8). But that woman wasn't the original Rosie. The woman in the poster was nameless. The poster was created by American graphic artist J. Howard Miller, probably for the Westinghouse Corporation's morale program. It appeared in early 1942. Americans would not be introduced to Rosie the Riveter until the following year.

In early 1943, a song titled "Rosie the Riveter" was released. The song was written by Redd Evans and John Jacob Loeb. Its lyrics included the following:

> All the day long,
>   Whether rain or shine,
> She's a part of the assembly line.
>   She's making history,
>   Working for victory,
> Rosie the Riveter.
>
> . . . .
> There's something true about,
>   Red, white, and blue about,
> Rosie the Riveter.

Several groups recorded "Rosie the Riveter." The song was very popular.

One of America's most famous illustrators soon created an image of Rosie the Riveter. For the cover of the May 29, 1943, issue of *The Saturday Evening Post*, Norman Rockwell painted the figure of a muscular young lady dressed in denim work overalls. This woman is clearly on her lunch break. She is seated, and in her left hand she holds a sandwich. Protective goggles are pushed

afford to see its military production drop off. Without a steady stream of new ships, planes, tanks, artillery pieces, and other equipment, the United States and the Allies couldn't win the war. The U.S. government urged women to take jobs in factories that produced military equipment. Millions

up on her forehead. A riveting gun rests across her lap. We know her name is Rosie because that is written on her lunch box.

Rosie is wearing stylish loafers rather than work shoes. Women's work shoes were hard to come by in the early years of the war. Her feet are on top of a tattered copy of *Mein Kampf*. That was a book written by Adolf Hitler, Nazi Germany's dictator. In the book, Hitler laid out his plans for German conquests. So symbolically, Rosie is trampling on Hitler's worn-out schemes to take over the world. When her lunch break ends, she'll be back on the assembly line, making the weapons that will defeat the enemy.

Mary Keefe, 78, stands next to Norman Rockwell's painting "Rosie the Riveter," in 2002. Keefe was a 19-year-old telephone operator in Arlington, Vermont, when she served as the model for Rockwell's classic 1943 work, which was commissioned for the cover of the *Saturday Evening Post*.

answered the call. As a group, these women became known as "Rosies." That nickname came from Rosie the Riveter.

Women who didn't take factory jobs found other ways to help America's war effort. Some enlisted in the armed services. They performed a variety of important non-combat tasks. Many married women who hadn't previously worked outside the home took jobs in stores and offices. This enabled them to support their families while their husbands were overseas fighting. Many women who didn't enter the workforce as a paid employee, volunteered in various capacities. Some joined civil defense groups, training to help protect their communities and respond to emergencies. Other women collected materials that could be recycled and used in the production of military equipment. These items included tin cans, scrap aluminum, and old tires. Even cooking fat, such as bacon grease, was saved. It could be used to make glycerol, a key ingredient in gunpowder.

As American men mobilized for war, the wives, mothers, and sisters they left behind at home would take on greater responsibility for supporting the war effort.

2

THE WOMEN AT HOME

Even before the war, housework was a full-time job. Not every home had a washing machine. In homes that did, women still needed to turn a hand crank to wring the water out of clothes. Then the clothes had to be hung out to dry. Everything had to be ironed before it could be worn.

Few homes had electric refrigerators. Instead, women bought large blocks of ice each day. The ice was put into an icebox to keep fresh food and milk from spoiling.

There were few prepackaged meals. Women had to make everything from ingredients they had on hand. A simple dinner could take hours to prepare. There were no microwaves or dishwashers to make life easier.

And life only got harder for women as the war went on. The needs of the armed forces came first. American factories and businesses stopped making goods for the home. Instead, they focused on producing items needed for the war effort. And the millions of American soldiers, marines, sailors, and airmen serving overseas had to be fed. That meant less beef, butter, coffee, sugar, and other food for the home front.

RATIONING

Of course, civilians had to eat, too. They needed clothes and shoes. They needed fuel.

American housewives line up to purchase their ration of sugar, circa 1942.

When goods are in short supply, the price tends to go up. Rich people can pay more for the goods they want. But people with less money might not be able to afford what they need. How could the government make sure important goods were fairly distributed?

The answer was rationing. Under this system, Americans could purchase only limited quantities of certain goods. Ration books were issued to every family and to individuals who lived alone. Inside were stamps that had to be turned in whenever certain items were bought. These items ranged from sugar, meat, and cheese to shoes, gas, kerosene, and car tires.

Despite the system of rationing, there were shortages. Stores often ran out of some items. Women might have to look in several stores to get what they wanted. But they could not drive far, because their gasoline was rationed, too. And rubber for tires was one of the first things to be in short supply.

A rack of rationed auto tires. Rubber was in short supply because in 1941, the Japanese had captured the Dutch East Indies, which produced 90 percent of the raw rubber used by American factories.

Clothing styles changed to use less fabric. But women felt the effect of clothing rationing most when dressing their children. Mending socks and patching knees only went so far. Growing children need bigger clothes and shoes.

Sheets for beds became scarce. Houses needed blackout curtains to hide their lights at night so that enemy planes wouldn't find their towns. How were women supposed to have cheerful homes with heavy black curtains in every window?

Meat rationing was a different problem. Farmers were producing plenty of meat, but most of it was going to the fighting men. While one pound of sugar is the same as another, one pound of steak is not the same as one pound of bacon. For these types of supplies, the government added point values to ration stamps. And some ration stamps were only usable during limited times. Like coupons today, they were not valid after a certain date. With rationing and points, shopping became very complicated. Women had to learn how to deal with the new realities quickly.

Metal was not used for non-war purposes. Nearly all canned, bottled, dried, and frozen vegetables, as well as all fruits, juices, and soups were rationed. Many people did not have reliable refrigeration for summer. In

FAST FACT

By the end of 1942, the U.S. government had issued gasoline-rationing stickers to all automobile owners. A black "A" sticker allowed the owner to buy four gallons of gas per week. It was issued to people for whom driving wasn't considered essential. A green "B" sticker, good for eight gallons per week, went to people who needed to drive for the war effort (for example, workers in weapons factories). Red "C" stickers were for physicians, ministers, mail carriers, and railroad workers. The amount of gas they could buy varied. Truckers supplying the population with needed goods had a "T" sticker, which enabled them to fill up whenever they needed.

the colder months, fresh foods were hard to get. Women had a hard time putting meals on the table, even when they could buy what they needed. But most Americans supported rationing, even though it made life more difficult. They believed that doing so would help win the war.

FARM TOWN, U.S.A.

On farms or in small towns, people could grow their own food. These home-makers could feed their families more easily during the war. In cities the government wanted people to grow their own food in "victory gardens." On small lots and parks and on rooftops, people planted gardens to supply themselves with food. In 1943, Americans on the home front grew 8 million tons of vegetables. Some men who were not serving in the military could help with gardening. But after harvest the women did most of the work. At the end of each growing season, they could preserve a lot of their food in glass jars by "canning" it. Home canners needed knowledge and skill. If they prepared preserves the wrong way, their jars of food could end up exploding on the shelf, or even poisoning their families.

In time, victory gardeners learned to plant foods that would keep without much care. Potatoes, carrots, onions, turnips, and hard-shelled squashes could be kept in a cool cellar for a year. They did not need to be canned or otherwise preserved.

WAR GARDENS FOR VICTORY

GROW VITAMINS AT YOUR KITCHEN DOOR

The U.S. government encouraged women to plant "victory gardens" and grow their own food. This would leave more food available for the soldiers fighting the war.

RECYCLING BY ANY OTHER NAME

Many factories that had once made new household items had switched to military production. Old things in the house had to be saved and reused. Broken stoves or refrigerators couldn't be replaced easily. Neither could rusty roller skates or bicycles. It was often up to women to make sure that tools were oiled so they wouldn't rust. Women had to be sure faucets were fixed so they didn't waste water heated with scarce fuel. Fuel was rationed based on the idea that houses should be heated only to 65°F in cold months. Some families heated only one or two rooms in their homes to save oil, coal, or electricity.

Movie star Rita Hayworth sacrificed her car bumpers to promote recycling of metal for the war effort.

Women saved many household items for collection drives, in almost the same way we recycle today. Among the things they saved were rags; animal bones; paper; metals, including tin cans, razor blades, and lipstick tubes; nylon stockings; and fats from cooking, which could be used to make explosives.

A woman wanted to look pretty, even during a war. But she could not have stockings. The silk and nylon was needed for parachutes. One wartime bride was happy to get a wedding present of a ration stamp for new shoes! A woman's makeup was also limited. The metal that had been used to make lipstick tubes and other makeup containers was used for guns and bullets. Beauty salons used toothpicks instead of metal hairpins.

They sewed hair curls in place with thread. They used thick paper instead of aluminum foil for coloring hair. When the government asked American women which cosmetics were most important in helping to keep their spirits up, women agreed that face powder, lipstick, rouge, and deodorants were the best. The government needed to be sure someone continued making those things.

MONEY

Women married to servicemen got a monthly check from the government. One wife who was pregnant and had a small child listed her budget in a letter to her husband:

Rent	$20.00
Elect[ricity]	$3.75
Tel[ephone]	$2.00
Milk	$6.50
Laundry	$4.00
Groceries	$30.00
insur[ance]	$2.95
Range oil	$2.80 (25 gal in summer)

	$72.00
Monthly Allowance	$80.00

That leaves a balance of $8.00 for clothing, medicine, heat in winter months, newspapers, periodicals, amusement, etc. Also there are bills, mostly contracted since your entry into the service, amounting to $45.00.

A serviceman's wife living only on his allotment would have a tough time of it. She might be looking at advertisements for women war workers with interest!

HOUSING

With sons and husbands gone, some women combined households. This helped them stretch their money and ration coupons further. Also, they could help each other with the chores and child care. But some women couldn't bear to leave their men. They followed them as long as they could while the men were stationed in the United States. This meant that towns near military bases became very crowded. It was hard for the women to find a place to stay while their husbands were on the base. They often had to share unpleasant places at high prices. For example, near Camp Polk in Alabama, young women—some with young babies—paid up to $50 a month to live in converted chicken coops, sheds, and barns. Thirty-five

ELEANOR ROOSEVELT

Eleanor Roosevelt was different from previous first ladies. She took a much more active role in promoting the policies of her husband, President Franklin D. Roosevelt. Mrs. Roosevelt often spoke about the concerns of ordinary Americans, whether they involved the hardships of the Depression or anxieties over the war. She connected readily with people. Americans found her reassuring as well as inspiring.

On December 8, 1941, the day after the Japanese attack on Pearl Harbor, Mrs. Roosevelt spoke to the nation in a radio broadcast. "I have a boy at sea on a destroyer—for all I know he may be on his way to the Pacific," she said.

> Two of my children are in coast cities in the Pacific. Many of you all over the country have boys in the service who will now be called upon to go into action; you have friends and families in what has become a danger zone. You cannot escape anxiety, you cannot escape the clutch of fear at your heart and yet I hope that the certainty of what we have to meet will make you rise above those fears. . . . I feel as though I were standing upon a rock and that rock is my faith in my fellow citizens.

people shared a single toilet and shower. In San Francisco, noted a city official in 1943, "families are sleeping in garages, with mattresses right on cement floors and three, four, five to one bed." People also lived in tents, basements, refrigerator lockers, and cars.

Women also gathered in port cities when their soldier or sailor was expected home for a quick leave, or when he might be passing through on his way overseas. "There is no place to put them," a newspaper reporter wrote. "The hotels put out cots in the halls or let them sleep uncomfortably in the chairs in the lobby."

Some landlords would not allow children on their properties. One hopeful mother placed the following advertisement in a New Orleans newspaper:

WANTED BY A NAVAL OFFICER'S WIFE—whose husband is serving overseas—and THREE MONSTERS in the form of my little children—TO RENT—a 2 or 3 bedroom house, apartment, BARN or CAGE or whatever is supposed to serve as shelter when such terrible creatures as children have to be considered.

The women at home during World War II didn't have it easy. But they cooperated with the rationing system. They were willing to do without. They did what was necessary to keep their households running in the absence of husbands and sons. And, in many cases, they did a whole lot more.

3

WOMEN VOLUNTEER

If a woman's place was in the home, her heart was with her men—husband, boyfriend, sons, and others. After the attack on Pearl Harbor, it seemed that everyone wanted to help the country. There was a rush to volunteer for every kind of home defense or civilian assistance program. Much of this was disorganized. And at first, women were often ignored. They were told that their job was to keep the home fires burning. They should let the men take care of things.

Many people, both men and women, joined local volunteer organizations. Sadly, many of these groups would never accomplish much. For example, some women got together and rolled bandages that could be used to treat wounded soldiers. However, that task could be done faster and under more germ-free conditions by machine. Other women baked cookies or knitted scarves and socks for servicemen.

Some women wanted to do even more to help. The two best-known organizations of volunteers during World War II were the Red Cross and the United Service Organizations, or USO. The USO helps keep up morale and sees to the welfare of the military and their families by offering recreation services. The American Red Cross responds to emergencies all over the country. Founded in 1881 by Clara Barton, it is part of a worldwide group that offers aid to the victims of war and other disasters.

THE USO

USO canteens are well known from World War II movie comedies and romances. Staffed by volunteer "hostesses," they could be a simple place for a tired off-duty soldier to have a cup of coffee. He (or she) could find a comfortable chair and some paper to write a letter back home. The canteens also could be places to meet the local girls and dance the night away. They had live

Young women volunteered to spend time with servicemen at USO clubs.

entertainment. Some volunteer organizations found it difficult to recruit as the war went on. But the USO could always count on young ladies. "New York agencies seeking girls to dance with servicemen . . . have waiting lists of more than 2,000 names," a reporter noted.

One mother of three sons in the navy wrote about her efforts with a Navy Mothers' Club. She worked with the local USO office. "They are giving a big Navy ball tonight for all the boys home on leave, and they are bringing 300 [men] from Auburn University who are there studying radio," the woman said.

> You bet, I'll be in my glory to be among all those sailors. . . . I'm taking about 35 of my girls [from the local USO] over. I think I'll be giving a dance at the club house for them too as Auburn isn't far away and [I can] entertain sailors for awhile, for I've certainly given my time for the soldiers. I carried a bunch of girls down to Fort Mitchell the other night.

It might seem that the USO's services weren't very important. But the USO played a vital role in keeping up the morale of servicemen. Many of them were still in their teens and had never before been far from home. Because local people could be suspicious of strangers, a USO-sponsored event gave citizens a chance to share a home-baked cookie and a smile with servicemen. Both went a long way toward helping homesick soldiers. An opportunity to dance to a swinging band might help a man forget his fears about the war for a little while.

The USO tried to extend its services to African-American servicemen. Segregation still existed in the military and in American society, so the USO sometimes provided separate clubs for black soldiers.

THE RED CROSS

The Red Cross, on the other hand, was more concerned with the health and welfare of people affected by war. It served its share of coffee and doughnuts, but it did much more. Long before the United States entered World War II, the American Red Cross was working in Europe. The American Red Cross got relief supplies from the International Red Cross in Geneva, Switzerland. It distributed these supplies to European civilians who were affected by the war.

By early 1941, American government officials recognized that the United States might become involved in the fighting. This would mean a big need for blood plasma for wounded soldiers. To prepare for that possibility, the Red Cross organized a blood donor program in the United States.

After the attack on Pearl Harbor, the Red Cross quickly swung into action in the United States. Paid staff and volunteers did the job assigned

FAST FACT

During the war years, the American Red Cross supplied 13.4 million pints of blood for military use. This blood came from 6.6 million donors. The Red Cross also provided 71,000 certified nurses to the military.

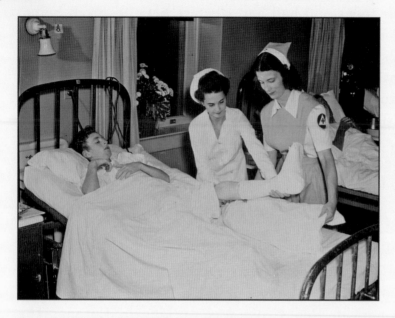

The Red Cross worked with the U.S. Office of Civilian Defense to train some 100,000 volunteers as nurse's aides. They were needed to work in civilian hospitals and health agencies. The trainee on the right is wearing a civil defense patch on her sleeve.

to the organization by Congress in 1905: to "furnish volunteer aid to the sick and wounded of armies in time of war" and to "act in matters of voluntary relief and in accord with the military and naval authorities as a medium of communication between the people of the United States of America and their Army and Navy."

The American Red Cross needed a large number of people to do its job. By the end of the war, more than 7.5 million volunteers were helping 39,000 paid staff members in more than 50 countries affected by the war. It's not known exactly how many Red Cross members were female. However, given that fewer men were available for volunteer work during the war, it's safe to say that women played a very large role. Of the 86 American Red Cross workers who lost their lives in World War II, 52 were women.

CIVIL DEFENSE

Some women found a useful role in preparing people on the home front for possible war-related emergencies. This is known as civil defense.

The American Women's Voluntary Services (AWVS) followed the example of a British volunteer group. It was founded in 1940 by Mrs. Alice Throckmorton McLean, a member of New York's high society. With the United States not yet involved in the war, many people made fun of Mrs. McLean's efforts. But within 18 months of its founding, the AWVS had 350,000 members in 350 units. Some units were as far away as Alaska and the Panama Canal Zone. They offered training in air-raid defense, fire fighting, motor mechanics, map reading, signal coding, and more.

The AWVS reached out to women from diverse groups. These included African Americans, Spanish speakers, Chinese Americans, and even members of the Native American Taos tribe. The AWVS chapter in New Orleans was racially integrated. The AWVS bridged class boundaries. It brought together women from all

This 1941 poster promotes an event for women in the New York area to learn about civil defense activities in which they can participate.

sorts of backgrounds. They were united by their determination to work together for a common cause.

The continental United States was spared from serious attack during World War II. For this reason, the AWVS wasn't needed for emergency response. Instead, members of the group sold war bonds, fed servicemen, helped wounded veterans, and organized and paid for desperately needed farm workers in California and Colorado. As doctors and health care work-

Uniformed members of the American Women's Voluntary Services, 1943.

ers became scarce, AWVS members took Red Cross training programs and staffed ambulances in New York City every day, around the clock.

SPECIAL GROUPS

Women volunteered in fields in which they had special skills. The WIRES represented the women in radio and electronics. WAMs were women aircraft mechanics. WOWs were women ordnance workers. The magazine *Ladies Home Journal* even organized its readers into WINS, Women in National Service. Chaired by 22 governors' wives, WINS asked women who couldn't take full-time war jobs to volunteer in school lunch programs. It asked them to help organize youth programs and to fill the need for labor in agriculture, day care, health care, home maintenance, and welfare agencies.

Every American woman, it seemed, wanted to do her part for the war effort. That included the three ladies, all of them over 70 years old, who made up the Ground Observers Corps for their New England district. These senior citizens did all the civil defense plane spotting there, 24 hours a day, seven days a week.

4

ROSIE THE RIVETER, WANDA THE WELDER, AND MORE

Between 1940 and 1943, approximately 4.4 million American women entered the workforce. They did almost every sort of work imaginable. Many—about 1.3 million—were farm workers. Women staffed hospitals. They did office work and other clerical jobs. They drove trains and trolley cars. They worked in restaurants and kitchens. Even the volunteer groups like the Red Cross and the USO needed paid workers, and women served in those jobs, too.

If women workers had many roles during the war, one is most remembered today: factory worker. Why is this the case? To begin, women hadn't previously done heavy work in hot, grimy factories. That had always been considered "men's work." But beyond that, the contributions of female factory workers during World War II were crucial. They played a big role in helping the Allies win the war.

Women had various reasons for deciding to work in a factory. Many women were motivated by patriotism. Others were attracted by the higher wages that factory jobs paid.

The work certainly wasn't easy. In fact, the pace could be grueling. Many women put in 48 hours a week, with just one day off. And that was before the frequent overtime shifts. But the hard work paid off. "For nine

A woman works on an airplane motor at the North American Aviation factory in California.

years before Pearl Harbor," noted the chairman of the U.S. War Production Board, "Germany, Italy and Japan prepared intensively for war, while as late as 1940 the war production of peaceful America was virtually nothing. Yet two years later the output of our war factories equaled that of the three Axis nations combined."

EXPLOSIVES WITH A WOMEN'S TOUCH

The Frankford Arsenal in Philadelphia was a major center for the manufacture of munitions. After the United States entered the war, the arsenal experienced a shortage of fuse-makers. This was skilled work. Time fuses had to be made to exacting standards. Otherwise, explosives would detonate too soon or too late. New fuse-makers typically required many months to train. But with a war on, there was a great need to churn out large quantities of fuses, and not enough time for training.

Arsenal managers tried to train new men quickly. But the results weren't good. Many of the fuses these men made had to be thrown out. So the arsenal tried something different. It hired women who were expert embroiderers. These women caught on fast. They could be trained to do the job in only 30 days.

Harriet Buono went to work at the arsenal at Picatinny, New Jersey, when she was 18 years old. Harriet came from a large family with no father. During the Depression, she'd quit school in the seventh grade to help support her 12 brothers and sisters by housecleaning. When the war started, the opportunity for better pay drew her to a munitions factory.

CHANGING PATTERNS IN THE WORKFORCE

World War II drew more American women than ever into work outside the home. By 1945, women made up 36 percent of the entire civilian labor force.

But the war changed more than the size of the female workforce. It also changed the composition. On average, women workers were now older than the previous workforce. They were also much more likely to be married. By war's end, one in every four married women was employed outside the home. For the first time in U.S. history, in fact, married women workers outnumbered single women workers.

Another new trend was the large number of mothers in the workforce. During the war years, about 1.5 million women with children under 10 years old held jobs outside the home. This created a big demand for childcare, which was hard to find.

She met her husband at a bowling alley while he was on leave from the army. After a short courtship, they got married one weekend. On Monday, it was back to the arsenal for Harriet. There she worked loading black powder into shells.

A munitions operator's job could be hazardous. The work was tedious and repetitive, and there wasn't much room for error. If a woman lost her focus, even for a brief period, the results could be deadly. Harriet Buono told an interviewer about how fatigue on a midnight shift almost had dire consequences for her. "Along about three or four o'clock in the morning," she recalled, "I don't know about you, but I couldn't keep my eyes open. . . . And fortunately for me, I only blew the machine up, and not my fingers. I fell asleep momentarily. That's the worst thing that happened to me during the war."

Others weren't so lucky. Munitions workers regularly suffered burns. Many lost fingers. Some even lost their lives on the job. In May 1943, for instance, explosions rocked a munitions factory in Elkton, Maryland. Fifteen workers were killed, and a hundred others were injured. It was

A woman war worker checks bomb cases at a factory in Omaha, Nebraska, 1944.

FAST FACT

Despite the addition of millions of women to the workforce, some areas of the country experienced labor shortages during World War II. There was talk of "drafting" women to work under a National Service Act. Six bills were introduced in Congress, but none ever came to a vote.

essential that "gunpowder girls" always approach their work with a careful and delicate touch.

WOMEN HAVE MUSCLE, TOO

Women worked in mines and warehouses. They worked in steel mills. They fought fires. All these jobs were necessary before a plane or tank or ship could be built. But with a war on, the women building those final products got most of the attention.

By 1943, approximately 475,000 women were working in aircraft factories. In huge buildings, the frame of an airplane started down a conveyor belt. By the time it reached the other end, hundreds of women had drilled, riveted, welded, bolted, wired, clamped, and otherwise put together a flying weapon. The aircraft plants were the size of small towns. They were incredibly noisy.

Because of their smaller size, women were especially valued for crawling into small spaces like the nose of a plane. A pair of riveters, one inside and one out, would scream instructions at each other over the noise. Women worked on every type of machinery, including the giant stamp presses that cut pieces of metal for the plane bodies. They also tested airplane engines, parts, and bomb-release mechanisms.

In 1939, before the war, a grand total of 36 women worked in American shipyards. By March of 1943, at least 23,000 women were helping build ships. At the end of 1944, the number topped 100,000. Women were able

Women worked at a variety of war-related jobs. (Top) Three women install fixtures in the tail section of a B-17 bomber. (Bottom left) a shipyard worker helps construct the S.S. *George Washington Carver*, launched in May 1943. (Bottom right) A technician checks electrical components at the Douglas Aircraft Company plant in California.

to transfer knowledge from their domestic lives to the workplace. Skills like patternmaking from sewing, or casting metal just like they made pastry. But they also operated drill presses, grinders, and lathes. They drove trucks, worked with sheet metal and electrical equipment, and staffed warehouses.

As was the case in the aviation industry, women in shipbuilding proved that, given the chance, they could do as much as their male coworkers. Toughness was a requirement. Women worked outdoors in all kinds of weather. They did dangerous work with hot metal. They were up on high scaffolds in icy winds.

"Our fingers get forever cut and bruised and infected from the incredible filth around us," shipyard worker Josephine Von Miklos noted. "We wear small and large bandages and we go on with the work."

WE *WILL* DO IT!

Whether motivated by patriotism, a need for money, a desire to learn new skills or something to keep their minds off their loved ones at war, the women of the United States rose to the challenge of manufacturing for the war economy. They did the job, and they did it well. The old stereotypes of fragile women in need of protection were beginning to fall away. The idea that women couldn't learn skills that were too demanding or complicated was proven wrong. A government publication from late 1942 summed it up:

> The [ship]yards were practically unanimous in reporting that on the whole the work done by women was considered equal to that of men. . . . Foremen . . . often found that women were quicker to learn than the men available. . . . Women exhibited a greater interest than did the men and were more anxious to know "why" and "how."

Women may have been doing the same work as men, but they weren't getting paid as much. In 1942, the National War Labor Board—a federal agency that was charged with resolving disputes between labor and industry—issued an order allowing employers to raise women's wages as much as necessary to bring them in line with men's. The automotive industry

A woman files small parts for an M5 anti-tank gun at the Vilter manufacturing plant in Milwaukee.

immediately raised women's base pay an average of 20 cents an hour. Yet overall, most women production workers still made about 40 percent less per week than men in the same position. How was this possible?

First of all, women had less seniority. What that means is they were the most recently hired people. The men had been working at their jobs longer and had been getting raises all that time. The women, even though they got their raises, didn't have time to catch up to the men. Also, having less seniority made it harder for women to be promoted to better, higher-paying jobs. It also meant they would be the first laid off if demand for the product slowed.

There were other ways women were kept from being paid as much as men. Some companies maintained separate seniority lists for men and

FAST FACT

Working with consultants from the University of Minnesota and the Mayo Clinic, Strato Equipment designed high-altitude pressure suits for pilots. Based in Minneapolis, Strato was a unique company. It was headed by a woman, and it employed only women. The only male presence at Strato was a department store dummy.

Female workers on the Chicago and North Western Railroad take a lunch break in their roundhouse in Iowa, spring 1943.

women. Some reclassified jobs formerly done by men as "women's jobs," and these jobs paid at a lower rate. Sometimes men received bonuses in addition to their regular wages, whereas women were paid straight hourly wages.

The country badly needed women in factories and in other jobs. Still, America wasn't ready to recognize how much women were worth in dollars and cents.

5

WOMEN IN THE SERVICES

On May 22, 1942, recruiting offices began to accept applications for officer candidates in the Women's Army Auxiliary Corps (WAAC). After a long struggle in Congress, a bill had finally passed that let women join an "auxiliary." This was a group that provided assistance to, but wasn't really a part of, the armed services.

Training camps sprang up across the country. The first was at an unused cavalry post left over from World War I. The second was located in Daytona Beach, Florida, where tourism was nonexistent thanks to gas rationing. Women rushed to join.

Would-be recruits with factory and government jobs needed the approval of government agencies to join the WAAC. That approval was often withheld. Their jobs were too important to the war effort. If these women persisted, they were generally made to wait up to 90 days before their application was considered.

WE WANT TO BE SOLDIERS!

Despite early enthusiasm for the WAAC program, many women weren't satisfied with an arrangement that only let them be auxiliaries. They wanted to be full members of the armed services. And the status of WAAC

Women's Army Corps recruits performed more than 150 jobs on bases away from the war zones, enabling male soldiers to go overseas and fight. Here, a WAC private named Mary Delession works on a vehicle engine at a miliary base in Idaho, 1943.

members as military auxiliaries concerned American leaders as well. The army could—and did—deploy members of the WAAC overseas. But because these women weren't full members of the armed forces, they did not receive the benefits or protections of regular soldiers. If captured by the enemy, for instance, they wouldn't be protected under international agreements governing the treatment of prisoners of war.

So in 1943, a new bill was introduced in Congress. This bill ended the WAAC and created the Women's Army Corps (WAC). Those who joined the WAC would be part of the real military.

Under its director, Oveta Culp Hobby, all WAC recruits received four weeks of basic training, during which they were closely supervised. After that, they trained in their specialties, living under less supervision. The trainees were aware that many people didn't think women would make good soldiers. So the trainees worked hard. They were proud of what they did.

WACs were sent all over the world. In October 1943, WACs arrived in India. November and December found WACs sent to Italy and Egypt. In January 1944, WACs were first deployed to the Pacific. They were used in non-combat jobs. Their work freed the men to fight the war.

OTHER BRANCHES FOLLOW

When the navy started the WAVES in late summer 1942, it sought to learn from the army's early mistakes in recruiting women. WAVES—Women Accepted for Volunteer Emergency Service—had "full military status with complete equality with men in the Navy." The WAVES had strict rules about who could join. The brightest women were recruited, and they trained on college campuses. Congress didn't allow the navy to send WAVES to other countries. WAVES served as secretaries and clerks. But they also served in the legal and medical areas, as well as in communications, science, technology, and aviation. By the end of the war, there were more than 8,000 female officers and 80,000 enlisted WAVES. Many stayed in the service after the war.

There is a funny story about the beginnings of women in the Marine Corps. At a dinner party on October 12, 1942, the commandant of the Marine Corps, Major General Thomas Holcomb, was asked, "What do you think about having women in the Marine Corps?" Before he could answer, a painting of the legendary Archibald Henderson, the marines' longest-serving leader, fell from the wall. Clearly, women marines would be a break with tradition. Even though some women had served in the Marines during World War I, that history had been forgotten by 1942.

At first, General Holcomb wasn't keen on the idea of women marines. But the island fighting in the Pacific required large numbers of marines. Holcomb needed to free up men who worked in the Marine Corps as office clerks, radio operators, drivers, mechanics, mess men (kitchen

WAVES march in formation at the U.S. Naval Training Center for women at the Bronx, New York.

workers), commissary clerks (store clerks), and so on.

General Holcomb decided that the women marines wouldn't need a special name. "They are Marines," he declared. "They don't have a nick-

OVETA CULP HOBBY: WAC LEADER

Oveta Culp was born in Killeen, Texas, in January 1905. Her father was a lawyer and state legislator. Her mother set an example of service to the community with charity work. A story about seven-year-old Oveta tells that she refused to sign a pledge not to drink liquor. While she had no interest in liquor when she was seven, she was afraid she might want to try it when she grew up. She didn't want to break a pledge.

Oveta read many of her father's law and government books as a young girl. At age 14, she went with him to the state capital of Austin. She became a very good speaker and was offered a job traveling the country. Her parents did not allow that, so she organized a group of teenaged musicians in her area. They traveled locally, giving performances to raise money for church organs.

At the age of 26, she married the 53-year-old former governor of Texas, William Hobby. He published the *Houston Post*, and through him she became interested in the newspaper business. Over the years, she learned how to edit, review books, and write editorials. Eventually, she took over as president and publisher of the *Post*.

After the attack on Pearl Harbor, Hobby was asked to come up with a plan for preparing women to assume non-combat roles in the army. This led to her appointment as head of the Women's Army Corps.

Hobby continued in public life after the war had ended. In 1953, President Dwight D. Eisenhower appointed her as secretary of the newly created Department of Health, Education, and Welfare. She also served on the board of directors for a variety of organizations, including the Corporation for Public Broadcasting. Oveta Culp Hobby died on August 16, 1995.

name and they don't need one. They get their basic training in a Marine atmosphere at a Marine post. They inherit the traditions of Marines. They are Marines."

In November 1942, President Roosevelt signed into law a bill creating the SPARS. This was the U.S. Coast Guard's Women's Reserve. About 12,000 women were recruited for the SPARS. They did most of the clerical work for the Coast Guard. Eventually other jobs were opened to them, including work with secret navigation systems and technical jobs.

WOMEN IN THE AIR

Women who were already trained pilots were eager to use their skills for the war effort. They were frustrated until September 1942. At that time, the Women's Auxiliary Ferrying Squadron (WAFS) was formed to deliver planes from the factories to military bases in the United States. Soon after, the Women's Flying Training Detachment (WFTD) began in Sweetwater, Texas. Women were taught to fly "the army way." They had uniforms, drills, and rules like the army. But they were never officially part of the military.

In August 1943, the WAFS and WFTD were joined together. They got a new name: the Women's Air Force Service Pilots (WASP). Throughout the war, they flew every type of military plane the United States produced. One heavy bomber, the B-29 Superfortress, had experienced a variety of mechanical problems during testing. At first, many male pilots were reluctant to fly the plane. So two WASP

A WASP pilot named Wilda Winfield flies a training mission at Frederick Army Air Field in Oklahoma.

These four female pilots were among many who were trained to ferry the B-17 "Flying Fortress" bomber from the United States to England, freeing up male pilots for combat.

pilots took a B-29 on a tour of U.S. airbases to prove it was safe.

WASP duties grew as the war went on. In addition to delivering planes, they towed targets for gunnery practice. They flew fighter planes close to the ground in training exercises for infantry soldiers. They became flight instructors. They tested repaired planes. They even worked as test pilots. WASP pilots flew a total of 60 million miles. Thirty-eight women were killed during their work.

NURSES IN THE MILITARY

While members of Congress and ordinary Americans alike worried about the proper role of women in the military, many seemed to forget an important fact. American women had been serving on or near battlefields since the nation's birth. Nurses cared for wounded soldiers from the Revolutionary War onward. But it wasn't until the Spanish-American War in 1898 that nurses began accompanying American soldiers overseas. And it wasn't until the early 1900s that the army and navy officially started nursing corps.

When the Japanese bombed Pearl Harbor, the Army Nurse Corps had fewer than 1,000 nurses. Six months later, it had 12,000. Very few of these recruits had any prior military experience. They went through four weeks of basic training in army nursing. Further training prepared army nurses for needed specialties such as anesthesiology.

American nurses take a break outside a field hospital in France, August 1944.

The military was desperate for nurses. And back home, fewer and fewer nurses were available for civilians. In June 1943, Congress passed the Bolton Act. It paid young women to go to nursing school. In return, they promised to become either public or military nurses after they graduated. Nursing schools also received government funds to speed up the education of nurses and to train nurses on the job. By the time this program ended in 1948, more than 150,000 new nurses had graduated.

Army nurses saw the war up close. "Right after D-Day in June 1944," recalled nurse Grace G. Patterson, "we were sent to France and landed on Utah Beach. When people argue about women being in combat, I think how silly they are, because we already were. In France we had 88mm artillery shells flying right over our heads."

Conditions were rough. The nurses traveled with the army. Sometimes they had to move at a moment's notice. "Crossing the English Channel in August 1944 was an experience I'll never forget," said Florence Heermance Wiechman:

> One hundred five nurses waited and waited on the dock, finally being told that all the cabins on the British ship were given out and we would sleep in the crews' mess hall, in the very bottom of the ship. . . . We slept in three layers, "Upper" was hammock, "Middle" was on the crude wooden mess tables, and "Lower" was on the floor. I drew a spot on the floor by an open pipe which dripped water and smelled like [a] sewer. . . .
>
> It took three days to cross a distance of twenty miles. . . . When we did land, it was about midnight, in a cold rain. Then we waited several hours for transportation, without either raincoats or bedrolls, resting in the wet sand.
>
> Our next stop was a cow pasture, literally. Being a city girl, it seemed wherever I turned there were cows in my way, even in the creek where we had to bathe and wash clothes.

Like the life of a soldier, the life of an army nurse often consisted of long periods of boredom followed by spurts of intense activity and horror. Nurses might have little to do for days or even weeks. But then, in the midst of a major battle, field hospitals would be swamped with wounded soldiers. At those times, nurses would work nearly nonstop trying to save

Women also reported on the war for major American publications. These war correspondents, photographed in London during 1943, include (left to right) Mary Welch (*Time* and *Life*), Dixie Tighe (*International*), Kathleen Harriman (*Newsweek*), Helen Kirkpatrick (*Chicago Daily News*), Lee Miller (*Vogue*), and Tania Long (*New York Times*).

lives. Fifty years later, army nurse Esther Edwards remembered her experiences during the Battle of the Bulge (December 1944–January 1945):

> Patients came by ambulance and helicopter all day and night. It was overwhelming. When I tried to rest, I couldn't sleep, thinking of all those wounded patients and all that needed to be done for them. There were some I cannot forget to this day, like one whose leg was amputated, and when he was told, he was so furious he wanted to die. There was little we could to do comfort him. Another man's jaw was nearly blown off and he needed more care than was available in our field hospital, so we hurriedly evacuated him to a larger one. Some developed kidney failure from shock and injuries, and died because there was nothing we could do for them there.

The military nurses who served in World War II helped save an untold number of lives. Over the course of the war, 201 nurses were killed.

6

AFTER THE WAR

What happened after the war was over? Many people assume that life in the United States basically returned to the way it had been before. The millions of American men who'd served in the armed forces came home and went back to their civilian jobs. The millions of American women who'd entered the workforce during the war years happily left their jobs. Married women resumed their roles as homemakers and mothers. Single women got married and started families in record numbers.

There is some truth in this picture. But it is at best an oversimplification.

The marriage rate did, in fact, start to climb again. By 1943, with American men off fighting the war, the marriage rate in the United States had dropped 10.3 percent. It fell again in 1944. The marriage rate rose in 1945 and exploded in 1946. A surge in the birthrate accompanied this trend. So it is true that as the soldiers came home, large numbers of women did marry and begin families.

It is also true that women left the factories in large numbers. Just as factories had retooled for war production in 1941 and 1942, they again had to retool for civilian production after the war. This meant that many factories closed down for a short time. They laid off their workers while they changed their machines to make products that would be needed in peacetime. When it was time to rehire, men who'd returned home from the war often took the jobs.

WHAT DID WOMEN THINK?

Millions of women had gone from relatively sheltered lives into the workplace. They'd learned to take care of themselves. Did they really want to go back to being housewives? Did they still feel a woman's place was in the home? Some women, no doubt, did. But the war had profoundly changed the attitudes of many women.

Typical was the sentiment expressed by a young woman who'd gone to work in an aircraft factory in California. "I guess I am capable of learning something that I never thought I would be able to do in a thousand years," she wrote to her boyfriend. "Oh I know you didn't do anything to discourage me but I was proving it to myself more than anything else so forgive [me] for bragging a little will you?"

Another woman—a "war bride" married in 1942—gave expression to her newfound sense of independence in a letter to her husband overseas:

> I must admit I'm not the same girl you left—I'm twice as independent as I used to be and to top it off, I sometimes think I've become "hard as nails"—hardly anyone can evoke any sympathy from me. No one wants to hear my troubles and I don't want to hear theirs. Also—more and more I've been living exactly as I want to and I don't see people I don't care about—I do as I . . . please.

Many women liked the satisfaction that work brought. And some weren't ready to give up their good-paying factory jobs. In Detroit, for example, a local union and a business decided to cancel the seniority that women workers had earned during the war. This would affect their pay, promotion, and retention rights. A small group of women "invaded" the union session and made sure that didn't happen.

Nonetheless, many women factory workers were forced to give up their jobs in favor of men. But that didn't mean women left the workforce entirely.

WOMEN IN THE POSTWAR WORKFORCE

In the postwar period, the female labor force was about two-thirds the size of its wartime peak. That means that a lot of women continued to work. What changed most, however, was the type of work women did.

In the two decades that followed the war, the United States saw a huge jump in its birthrate. The years 1946–1964 are known as the "baby boom." The growing numbers of children created a big demand for certain occupations. To begin, someone had to teach all the kids. Women filled most of the teaching jobs, especially at the elementary school level. More nurses were needed to look after the health of the country's children. Again, it was women who took the vast majority of the nursing jobs.

Changes in health care also fueled increased demand for nurses. Doctors now had penicillin to fight infections. Hospitals were able to successfully treat people who would have died before. And in the 1940s and 1950s, health insurance became widely available. The government encouraged companies to offer health insurance to their workers. Unions argued for health insurance when they negotiated contracts for the workers they represented. So medical care was improving, and there was money available to pay for it. Large numbers of women would find employment on hospital staffs as well as in health insurance companies.

During the war years, women had shown they were skilled office workers. They were used in business, in industry, and in the military to do paperwork. Before the war, many of these clerical jobs had been done by men. Now the jobs were open to women. Greater numbers of women also started taking on work as accountants, bookkeepers, bank tellers, and in other white-collar occupations.

DEMOBILIZING WOMEN IN THE MILITARY

The WASP was deactivated in December 1944. Because it was never officially part of the military, its pilots weren't able to benefit from veterans' programs such as the G.I. Bill. The G.I. Bill provided loans to, and paid the education expenses of, veterans.

The U.S. Air Force became an independent branch of the military in 1947. Previously, it had been part of the army. For 20 years, the U.S. Air Force offered only non-flying positions to females. Beginning in 1977, however, women were permitted to become air force pilots. That same

Female sailors are inspected at a San Diego naval base. Today, women make up about 20 percent of the U.S. armed forces.

year, WASP members finally became eligible for veterans' benefits. They didn't begin to receive military honors until 2002.

The WAC saw its numbers decline dramatically after the war. By 1950, women represented only 1 percent of the army. Recruiting was affected by several factors, including rising civilian salaries, with which the army couldn't compete. The army also required women to have higher levels of education than men in order to enlist. Yet until the late 1960s, the jobs available for women in the army were limited mostly to clerical and secretarial work.

The Coast Guard's SPARS were disbanded after the war. The 12,000 women reservists were released.

The Women's Marine Reserve was to be disbanded in September 1946. But that spring, a campaign was started to keep some women marines, and the order was changed. A small peacetime Women's Marine Reserve would be maintained. Its members would perform clerical duties. As time went on, the planned number of members in the Women's Marine Reserve grew from 100 to 300. Many male marines now believed that the women had a vital role to play in the Marine Corps. Among them was General Thomas Holcomb, the commandant who'd earlier expressed his doubts. "Like most Marines," General Holcomb admitted, "when the matter first came up I

The trend of greater female participation in the labor force has continued. According to the most recent statistics from the U.S. Department of Labor, today women make up 47 percent of the labor force.

didn't believe women could serve any useful purpose in the Marine Corps. . . . Since then I've changed my mind."

A NEW WOMAN

Even before the war had ended, people wondered whether women would be willing to give up their jobs. They remembered the Great Depression, when there wasn't enough work for everyone. They were afraid there would be no jobs for the men when they came home from the war. In 1944, Eleanor Roosevelt asked a government official, "Will women want to keep their jobs after the war is over?" The answer she got was this:

> Married women usually keep their jobs only when they have real need for money at home. This, of course, does not mean that women who take up some kind of work as a career will not stay in that work if they like it, whether they are married or single.

It seemed that the idea of working women was starting to gain acceptance. Also, instead of an economic depression, the soldiers returned to a booming economy. Years of doing without had passed. Newly married couples with young children needed places to live. They needed furniture and things for their new houses. There were plenty of jobs to go around. Women who wanted to work could find jobs, especially if they had the right skills. Mrs. Roosevelt spoke to that as well:

> The first obligation of government and business is to see that every man who is employable has a job, and that every woman who needs work has it. A woman does not need a job if she has a home and a family requiring her care and a member of the household is earning an adequate amount of money to maintain a decent standard of living. If however there is a margin of energy left in men or women and they want to put it into bettering their standard of living, . . . they should have the opportunity. We should gear our economy to a place where we can give all people who desire to work . . . a chance to work on something which gives them creative satisfaction.

A better standard of living would become the goal of most families. And as people wanted more, they needed more money. This would give women more reason to work.

At the same time, as more laborsaving appliances came into use, housekeeping was taking less time. It was more possible for women to have a job and run a household. The world was changing, and so was women's role.

A year after the war ended, nearly 2.2 million women were laid off. The proportion of women in the labor force had dropped from 36 percent to 29 percent. But that was still higher than in 1940, when women made up 25.5 percent of the labor force. So even with the pressures to resume their traditional role as homemakers, women were still holding their own at work.

FAST FACT

In the United States, men continue to be paid more than women. Overall, women earn just 77 cents for every dollar earned by men.

CHAPTER NOTES

p. 12:   "dominate and enslave . . ." Franklin D. Roosevelt, *Rendezvous with Destiny: Addresses and Opinions of Franklin Delano Roosevelt*, ed. J. B. S. Hardman (New York: The Dryden Press, 1944), p. 167.

p. 12:   "great arsenal of democracy," Roosevelt, *Rendezvous with Destiny*, p. 170.

p. 22:   "Rent $20.00 . . ." Reid, Marjorie quoted in Judy B. Litoff and David C. Smith, *Since You Went Away: World War II Letters from American Women on the Home Front* (New York: Oxford University Press, 1991), p.105.

p. 23:   "I have a boy at sea . . ." Eleanor Roosevelt, quoted in Richard Lingeman, *Don't You Know There's a War On?: The American Home Front, 1941–1945* (New York: Thunder's Mouth Press, 2003), p. 27.

p. 24:   "families are sleeping in garages . . ." Lingeman, *Don't You Know There's a War On?*, p. 81.

p. 24:   "There is no place . . ." H. H. Smith, "Port of Navy Wives" *Collier's Weekly* (February 20, 1943).

p. 24:   "WANTED BY A NAVAL . . ." quoted in "Whither Thou Goest," *Time* (August 30, 1943), p. 68.

p. 26:   "New York agencies seeking girls . . ." J.C. Furnas, "Are Women Doing Their Share?" *Saturday Evening Post* (April 29, 1944), p.42.

p. 26:   "They are giving a . . ." Litoff and Smith, *Since You Went Away*, p. 190.

p. 28:   "furnish volunteer aid to the sick . . ." quoted in "World War II Accomplishments of the American Red Cross," http://www.redcross.org/museum/history/ww2a.asp

p. 31:   "For nine years before . . ." Donald Nelson, "What Industry Did," in *While You Were Gone: A Report on Wartime Life in the United States*, ed. Jack Goodman (New York: Simon & Schuster, 1946), p 213.

p. 34:   "Along about three or four . . ." Harriet Buono, interviewed for "Rosie the Riveter: Morris County Women During World War II," www.archive.ccm.edu/rosie/HBtranscript.htm

p. 37: "Our fingers get forever cut . . ." Josephine Von Miklos, *I Took a War Job* (New York: Simon and Schuster, 1943), p. 195.

p. 37: "The [ship]yards were practically unanimous . . ." quoted in "Employment of Women in Shipyards," *Monthly Labor Review* (February 1943), p. 280.

p. 43: "full military status with complete equality . . ." quoted in "WAVES," *Time* (August 10, 1942), p. 71.

p. 43: "What do you think about having women . . ." Mary V. Stremlow, *Free a Marine to Fight: Women Marines in World War II* (Washington, D.C.: Marine Corps Historical Center, 1994), p. 1.

p. 44: "They are Marines . . ." Stremlow, *Free a Marine to Fight*, p. 2.

p. 48: "Right after D-Day . . ." Grace G. Patterson, quoted in Diane Burke Fessler, *No Time For Fear: Voices of American Military Nurses in World War II* (East Lansing: Michigan State University Press, 1996), p. 169.

p. 48: "Crossing the English Channel . . ." Florence H. Wiechman, quoted in Fessler, *No Time For Fear*, p. 214.

p. 49: "Patients came by ambulance . . ." Esther Edwards, quoted in Fessler, *No Time For Fear*, p. 100.

p. 51: "I guess I am . . ." Litoff and Smith, *Since You Went Away*, p. 157.

p. 51: "I must admit I'm . . ." Litoff and Smith, *Since You Went Away*, p. 4.

p. 53: "Like most Marines, when the matter . . ." Mary V. Stremlow, *Free a Marine to Fight: Women Marines in World War II* (Washington, D.C.: Marine Corps Historical Center, 1994), p. 40.

p. 54: "Will women want to keep . . ." Eleanor Roosevelt, "Woman's Place After the War," *Click* (August 1944), pp. 17, 19.

p. 54: "Married women usually keep their jobs . . ." Ibid.

p. 55: "The first obligation of government . . ." Ibid.

CHRONOLOGY

1939   On September 1, Germany invades Poland, touching off World War II.

1940   In a December speech, President Roosevelt declares "We must be the great arsenal of democracy." American factories gear up to produce military supplies.

1941   In March, the Lend-Lease Bill is passed; on December 7, the Japanese attack the American naval base at Pearl Harbor, Hawaii. The United States declares war the following day.

1942   In May, Congress creates the Women's Auxiliary Army Corps (later, the WAC) under the direction of Oveta Culp Hobby; Gasoline rationing begins; the Lanham Act permits federal grants and loans for childcare programs. It is hoped this will ease the strain on working mothers in war industries; the Women Accepted for Voluntary Emergency Services (WAVES) program is authorized by Congress in July; in September, the Women's Air Force Service Pilots (WASPS) is established. It will provide the services with more than 1,000 additional pilots; in December, coffee rationing begins.

1943   In February, shoe rationing begins. Civilians are permitted three pairs of shoes a year; in March, meat rationing begins; in April, the rationing of fats (oil, lard, butter), canned goods, and cheese begins. To stop rising prices (inflation) President Roosevelt freezes wages, salaries, and prices; the *Saturday Evening Post* prints the "Rosie the Riveter" cover in May; the Bolton Bill is passed in Congress. It provides federal funds to help train more nurses.

1944   In May, most meat rationing ends; on June 6—D-day—American and Allied troops invade France.

1945   In May, Germany surrenders, ending the war in Europe; Japan surrenders in August, bringing World War II to an end.

FURTHER READING

FOR YOUNGER READERS

Coleman, Penny. *Rosie the Riveter: Women Working on the Home Front in World War II*. New York: Crown, 1995.

Corrigan, Jim. *The 1940s Decade in Photos: A World at War*. Berkeley Heights, N.J.: Enslow Publishers, 2010.

Donnelly, Karen. *American Women Pilots of World War II*. New York: Rosen, 2004.

Peterson, Claire. *Rosie the Riveter*. New York: Scholastic, 2009.

Price, Sean Stewart. *Rosie the Riveter: Women in World War II*. Mankato, Minn.: Heinemann Raintree, 2008.

FOR OLDER READERS

Colman, Penny. *Rosie the Riveter: Women Working on the Home Front in World War II*. New York: Crown, 1998.

Hartmann, Susan M. *Home Front and Beyond: American Women in the 40's*. Boston: Twayne Publishers, 1982.

Lingeman, Richard. *Don't You Know There's a War On?: The American Home Front 1941–1945*. New York: Thunder's Mouth Press, 2003.

Litoff, J. B., and D. C. Smith. *Since You Went Away: World War II Letters from American Women on the Home Front*. New York: Oxford University Press, 1991.

Nathan, Amy. *Yankee Doodle Gals: Women Pilots of World War II*. Washington, D.C.: National Geographic, 2001.

Stevens, M.E., ed. *Women Remember the War: 1941–1945*. Madison, WI: Wisconsin Historical Society, 1993.

INTERNET RESOURCES

www.history.com/topics/rosie-the-riveter

The History Channel's page has links to videos of women working in war industries as well as women in the military.

www.nwhm.org/online-exhibits/partners/exhibitentrance.html

"Partners in Winning the War: American Women in World War II" is an outstanding online exhibit from the National Women's History Museum.

www.nps.gov/pwro/collection/website/home.htm

This site, from the National Park Service, features the first-person stories of more than 20 women who worked in defense-related jobs during World War II.

www.pophistorydig.com/?p=877

A multifaceted look at the "Rosie the Riveter" story, with explanatory text, posters, photos, song lyrics, and more.

www.history.army.mil/books/wwii/72-14/72-14.HTM

The story of the Army Nurse Corps in World War II.

GLOSSARY

arsenal—a place where weapons and ammunition are made.

auxiliary—giving assistance or support; a group that gives assistance or support.

black market—illegal trade in goods.

civil defense—a system for protecting life and property (especially during wartime) that depends on civilian volunteers.

dictatorship—a form of government in which absolute power is held by one person or a small group.

economy—the system by which goods and services are produced, distributed, and consumed in a country or other geographic region.

Great Depression—a period of economic crisis that lasted from about 1939 until the beginning of World War II.

munitions—weapons and ammunition.

ordnance—military materiel, such as weapons, ammunition, combat vehicles, and equipment.

penicillin—the first antibiotic discovered, used to treat a wide range of infections.

rationing—a system for fairly distributing a limited supply of goods by restricting the amount any person may purchase.

recruit—to enroll new members; to secure the services of.

retool—to change what a factory can make by putting in new machinery and tools. seniority—privileged status (for example, better pay, better hours, first claim at a better position within a company) earned by longer service.

union—an organization of workers formed to bargain with an employer.

INDEX

Air Force, 52–53
  See also military
aircraft factories. *See* factory
  work
American Red Cross. *See*
  Red Cross
American Women's
  Voluntary Services
  (AWVS), 29–30
Army Nurse Corps, 47
  See also nurses

Barton, Clara, 25
birthrate, postwar, 50, 52
blood donor program, 27–28
  See also Red Cross
Bolton Act, 48
Buono, Harriet, 33–34

civil defense groups, 16,
  28–30
Coast Guard. *See* U.S.
  Coast Guard's Women's
  Reserves (SPARS)

economy, postwar, 54–55
Edwards, Esther, 49
Eisenhower, Dwight D., 44
Evans, Redd, 14

factory work, 12, 13, 15–16,
  31–39, 50, 51
  and injuries, 34–35, 37
  and wages, 37–39
Frankford Arsenal, 32–33
fuse-making, 32–33
  See also munitions manufacturing

G.I. Bill, 52
Great Depression, 10, *11*,
  13, 54
Ground Observers Corps,
  30

Henderson, Archibald, 43
Hitler, Adolf, *12*, 15
Hobby, Oveta Culp, 42, 44
Holcomb, Thomas, 43,
  44–45, 53–54
housework, 17, 19–20, 55
housing, 22–24

International Red Cross, 27
  See also Red Cross

jobs (for women), 10,
  14–15, 31, 51, 52
  See also factory work;
  military
journalists, women, *49*

Keefe, Mary, *15*
Kirkpatrick, Helen, *49*

Lend-Lease Act, 12–13
Loeb, John Jacob, 14
Long, Tania, *49*

Marine Corps, 43–45, 53–54
  See also military
marriage rate, postwar, 40
married women, 10, 16, 33
McLean, Alice
  Throckmorton, 29
military
  and demobilization of
  women, 52–54

Marine Corps, 43–45,
  53–54
nurses in the, 47–49
SPARS (Coast Guard),
  45, 53
Women Accepted for
  Volunteer
  Emergency Service
  (WAVES), 43
Women's Air Force
  Service Pilots
  (WASP), 45–46,
  52–53
Women's Army Auxiliary
  Corps (WAAC), 41
Women's Army Corps
  (WAC), 42, 44, 53
Women's Auxiliary
  Ferrying Squadron
  (WAFS), 45
Women's Flying Training
  Detachment
  (WFTD), 45
Women's Marine
  Reserve, 53–54
Miller, J. Howard, 14
Miller, Lee, *49*
munitions manufacturing,
  12, 13, 15–16, 31–35, *38*
  See also factory work

National Service Act, 35
National War Labor Board,
  37
navy, 43
  See also military
Navy Mothers' Club, 26
nurses, 27, *28*, 52
  in the military, 47–49

Numbers in **bold italics** refer to captions.

Patterson, Grace G., 48
pay. *See* wages
Pearl Harbor, 13, 23, 47
    See also World War II

rationing, 17–20, 24
recycling, 16, 21–22
Red Cross, 25, 27–28, 30, 31
Rockwell, Norman, 14–15
Roosevelt, Eleanor, 23, 54, 55
Roosevelt, Franklin D., 11, 12, 23, 45
Rosie the Riveter, 14–16

seniority, 38–39, 51
shipyards, 35, *36*, 37
    See also factory work
SPARS (Coast Guard), 45, 53
Strato Equipment, 38

Tighe, Dixie, *49*

United Service
    Organizations (USO), 25–27, 31
U.S. Coast Guard's Women's
    Reserves (SPARS), 45, 53
    See also military

victory gardens, 20
volunteering, 16, 25

and civil defense groups, 28–30
and the Red Cross, 25, 27–28, 31
and the United Service
    Organizations
    (USO), 25–27, 31
Von Miklos, Josephine, 37

wages
    inequality in, 37–39, 55
    military, 22
WAMs (women aircraft mechanics), 30
war effort
    and civil defense groups, 16, 28–30
    and rationing, 17–20, 24
    and volunteering, 16, 25, 27–31
"We Can Do It!" (poster), 8–9, 14
Welch, Mary, *49*
Wiechman, Florence
    Heermance, 48
WINS (Women in National Service), 30
WIRES, 30
Women Accepted for
    Volunteer Emergency
    Service (WAVES), 43
Women's Air Force Service
    Pilots (WASP), 45–46, 52–53

Women's Army Auxiliary
    Corps (WAAC), 41–42
    See also Women's Army
    Corps (WAC)
Women's Army Corps
    (WAC), 42, 44, 53
Women's Auxiliary Ferrying
    Squadron (WAFS), 45
Women's Flying Training
    Detachment (WFTD), 45
Women's Marine Reserve, 53–54
workforce
    number of women in, 9, 31, 33, 35, 51, *54*, 55
    postwar, 51
World War II
    America's entrance into, 13–16
    beginning of, 10, *12*
    and the Lend-Lease Act, 12–13
    and neutrality of U.S., 11–13
    and Pearl Harbor, 13, 23, 47
    See also military; war
    effort
WOWs (women ordnance workers), 30

CONTRIBUTORS

DONNA ROPPELT worked with Deaf children for over 30 years. Before that, she worked in factories, stores, offices, and warehouses. She even tried to enlist once. She wants the history of the United States to be accessible to everyone who wants to learn about it.

Senior Consulting Editor **A. PAGE HARRINGTON** is executive director of the Sewall-Belmont House and Museum, on Capitol Hill in Washington, D.C. The Sewall-Belmont House celebrates women's progress toward equality—and explores the evolving role of women and their contributions to society— through educational programs, tours, exhibits, research, and publications.

The historic National Woman's Party (NWP), a leader in the campaign for equal rights and women's suffrage, owns, maintains, and interprets the Sewall-Belmont House and Museum. One of the premier women's history sites in the country, this National Historic Landmark houses an extensive collection of suffrage banners, archives, and artifacts documenting the continuing effort by women and men of all races, religions, and backgrounds to win voting rights and equality for women under the law.

The Sewall-Belmont House and Museum and the National Woman's Party are committed to preserving the legacy of Alice Paul, founder of the NWP and author of the Equal Rights Amendment, and telling the untold stories for the benefit of scholars, current and future generations of Americans, and all the world's citizens.